MALI

Land of Gold & Glory

FIVE PONDS PRESS

WEST PALM BEACH, FL

Between the years 1200 and 1500
the Kingdom of Mali was one of the richest
in the world, yet few Americans have heard of it.
Learn the truth.
Meet its great leaders.
Share the story of an awesome civilization.

Five Ponds Press books are available at a special discount when purchased in bulk for educational use. Contact Special Sales Dept. at Five Ponds Press or e-mail: info@fivepondspress.com

The author gratefully acknowledges the contributions of Dr. Barbara B. Brown and Professor Pilar Quezzaire-Belle of Boston University's African Studies Center and wishes to express her appreciation for the encouragement of the Hanover County (VA) Public Schools.

Special thanks to Bree Linton, Lara Samuels, Kathy Morrison, Don Zeigler, and Anita Parker.

Book design: Joy Masoff

This modern day Fulani girl is dressed for a special occasion. The Fulani are one of many ethnic groups in Western Africa.

Table of Contents

Chapter One

KEEPERS OF THE PAST

The secrets of times gone by

HISTORY LIVES!

This man is a famous GRIOT. You can read about griots on these pages. He's playing a KORA, a 21-string instrument that sounds like a cross between a guitar and a harp. He sings of great people and events of the past.

A very wrinkled old man sits by the river's edge. The sun is setting, and the burning heat of the day has turned cooler. The sky explodes with color. The old man clears his throat and begins to speak.

"Come closer. Listen to my tale. It is a story of a mighty king and the rich lands he ruled. It is a story of gold and salt. It is a story of a great city, almost lost in the sands of the desert…and a way of life almost lost in the sands of time."

The old man sips water from a gourd, the empty shell of a dried melon. His eyes are as bright as the setting sun. And he calls out…

*"I am a **griot** (GREE-oh)—a teller of stories and singer of history. I am the keeper of memories and laws. I am the teacher of kings. I hold the whole story of my country in my head and in my heart. My father was a griot, and my grandfather, and his grandfather before him.*

*This is the story of a great empire, Mali, and the **Mande** (MAHN-day) peoples who lived there. It is the story of a time when Mali was a rich and powerful place—a land of palaces and gold. Some called it the Bright Country, and that was the way it was—a bright and shining place."*

The sun slips lower. The sky glows. The griot picks up his *kora* and softly strums the strings. As he speaks, the years slip away, and today becomes a thousand yesterdays.

Proud Africa was the place where human life began almost a million years ago. About 8,000 years ago people began to appear in the western parts of Africa, a place of great natural richness. Today that land sits at the edge of a huge desert called the **Sahara** (Sa-HA-rah)—a three million-square-mile sandbox.

The empire of Mali lay to the south of the Sahara, in an area called the **sahel** (sah-HEL), which means "shore." Here there was enough rainfall to nourish scrubby grasslands and **savannahs** (suh-VA-nuhz), where the grass grows taller. Today the climate has changed and it is much drier, but back then there was fine soil where crops could grow. Fields of millet (a kind of grain) dotted the land. There were huge gold deposits in the forests to the west and south of the empire and there were vast salt mines in the north.

In this land of richness, several large clans grew. A clan is like a very big family with lots of cousins, aunts, uncles, and close friends all living next to each other.

But there was one problem—a big problem!

The clans did not get along with one another and fought all the time. People were getting hurt and dying.

The Sahara desert covers more than 3.5 million square miles (9 million sq. km). That's almost the size of the continental United States!

Since it is never good to fight, the clans finally decided to join together. The clan leaders sat down and chose a **mansa** (MAN-suh)—one person who would rule over all of them.

In time their mansa became rich and powerful. Other kings followed, and cities rose up in the heart of West Africa—cities that grew into empires.

The old griot smiles, then says, "*Empires are born, and kings live, then die. But the legends of these mighty rulers last forever. That is my job...to share the stories of great and wonderful people.*"

In modern-day Mali thirsty cattle drink after a long walk across the savannah. Raising herds of cattle first became possible in the 1400s, after a climate change killed off deadly tsetse flies .

Chapter Two

WHERE IS MALI?

A land in the sand

Africa is a huge continent—more than three times the size of the U.S.A. When you think of Africa, you might think of lions, elephants, and rainforests, but there is much more to Africa than that. You now know a little about the sahel and its grasslands, but did you know that 800 years ago a brave man led his people to freedom and built a great nation?

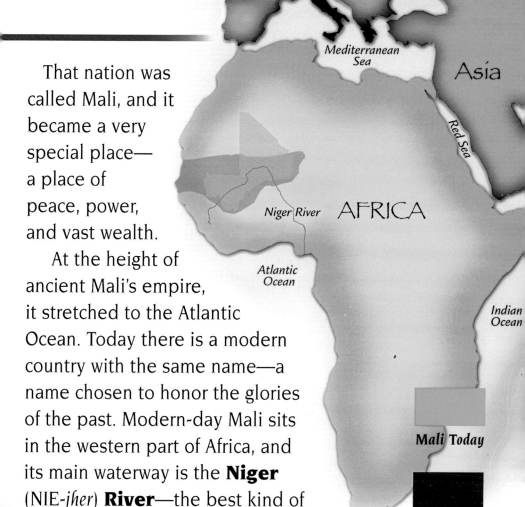

That nation was called Mali, and it became a very special place— a place of peace, power, and vast wealth.

At the height of ancient Mali's empire, it stretched to the Atlantic Ocean. Today there is a modern country with the same name—a name chosen to honor the glories of the past. Modern-day Mali sits in the western part of Africa, and its main waterway is the **Niger** (NIE-*jher*) **River**—the best kind of "road" that can exist in the sand and savannah. This watery highway helped to make Mali great.

Europe

Mediterranean Sea

Asia

Red Sea

Niger River

AFRICA

Atlantic Ocean

Indian Ocean

Mali Today

Empire of Mali in 1330

In this modern Mali brick yard, bricks are still made as they were a thousand years ago, from mud and straw that is left to bake in the sun.

The Niger is one of the great rivers of the world. It stretches over 2,500 miles (4,000 km)—the distance from Washington D.C. to California.

Mali sits along a big curve in the river, where it splits into a vast inland **delta**. A delta is a place where a river (which carries a lot of soil in its waters) slows down, leaving large deposits of rich dirt along its banks.

The Niger brings Mali life-giving water and fertile soil to grow crops. It forms a watery roadway for boats to travel along from town to town. The Niger River curves north in Mali, bringing the river closer to the Sahara (and Europe and Asia) than at any other place along its path.

Towns grew along its rich river banks, and soon those towns grew into cities. It was here that great centers of trade began to grow.

The Niger River curves around the city of Djenne.

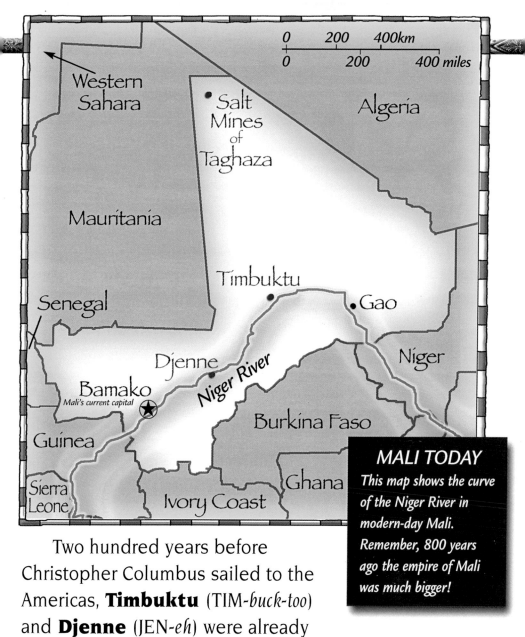

0   200   400km

0   200   400 miles

Western
Sahara

• Salt
Mines
of
Taghaza

Algeria

Mauritania

Timbuktu

• Gao

Senegal

Djenne

Niger

Bamako
Mali's current capital ★

Niger River

Guinea

Burkina Faso

Sierra
Leone

Ivory Coast

Ghana

MALI TODAY
*This map shows the curve
of the Niger River in
modern-day Mali.
Remember, 800 years
ago the empire of Mali
was much bigger!*

Two hundred years before
Christopher Columbus sailed to the
Americas, **Timbuktu** (TIM-*buck-too*)
and **Djenne** (JEN-*eh*) were already
mighty cities. They were built along an important trade
route that brought the riches of West Africa north
toward Europe. For hundreds of years, these cities
prospered, and their fame spread.

Why? Mali had something that everyone wanted—
gold! And it had something everyone needed—salt!

Chapter Three

SALT & GOLD

The treasures that built an empire

Our bodies need salt to survive. Early people got the salt their bodies needed by eating the raw meat of animals they hunted. When people turned to farming instead of hunting for food, the grains they grew did not have enough salt. That's when salt became valuable.

Back then there were no refrigerators. Salt kept food from spoiling. It made food that was starting to spoil taste okay.

THE SALT MINES

This modern-day salt seller squats next to salt slabs from the salt mines at Taghaza. Taghaza was a terrible place to work, an oven-on-Earth where temperatures could reach 135°. In times past only slaves would work there. It was a certain death sentence. They even lived in houses made of salt.

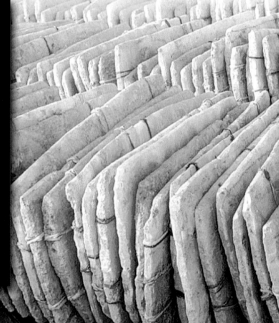

Salt is still used to tan leather and to make medicines. In the heat of the West African sun, where people sweat all day, salt keeps the body from losing too much water. Salt means the difference between life and death.

One hundred years ago some places in Africa still used salt as money. In Mali salt was so precious that it was traded for gold.

Gold might seem like the exact opposite of salt. Today there is salt in every supermarket. But you will not find gold in *any* supermarket!

Gold has been treasured for thousands of years. Why? Gold is a beautiful thing to see. Because it is easy to mold, gold can be formed into coins and jewelry. It is easier to pay someone with a gold coin than with a pig or a cow. Gold lasts a long time. The only problem is that there is very little of it in the world. People always want rare things. Back in the year 1000, both salt and gold were rare and in great demand.

Mali controlled the trade of both!

Life was very different 800 years ago. There were no shopping malls and no jet planes. There were no trains and trucks to move products from here to there.

Instead, every day as the sun began to rise in North Africa, long lines of camels loaded down with all sorts of goods began to make their slow, steady way across the the Sahara to Mali's great markets. The **caravans** (CAIR-*uh-vans*) brought treasures from as far away as China—jewels and silks, furs and rare birds—anything and everything to trade for gold and salt. South of the desert, boats waited to carry goods along the rivers.

People were traded too. Slavery has been around for many thousands of years in all parts of the world. When wars were fought, captured soldiers became slaves. When towns were conquered, their people were sometimes forced into slavery. Instead of going to jail, many criminals became slaves.

The caravans traveled about three miles an hour. Sometimes they traveled by starlight in the cool of the desert night. They had to survive sandstorms, dried-up wells, scorpions, and temperatures that hit 130° F. Still, the caravans came because gold is so very valuable!

Camels get ready to cross the Sahara as the blazing desert sun sets.

Camels were the trucks and trains of the Sahara trade routes because camels were built for life in the desert. They have two rows of eyelashes to shield their eyes from sand and sun. They can drink twenty-five gallons of water at a time! Their wide hooves don't sink in the sand like horses' hooves do.

In a land with few or no roadways, camels helped make ancient Mali rich, for on their humped backs they carried all the treasures of the world.

PLAY THE TRADING GAME

Cut pieces of colored paper into squares—four blues, six reds, six greens, six yellows, one gold, and one white—for each group of 3-4 children.
Blue paper=water
Red paper=meat
Green paper=fruit and veggies
Yellow paper=bread
White paper=salt
Gold paper=gold

Break up into groups of three or four. Place the squares in a small bag and take turns drawing out a square one at a time.

When all the squares have been drawn, start trading them with your friends, trying to collect at least one object of each color.

Remember that if you have gold but no water, you cannot live. If you have meat but no salt, your meat will not last very long. If you need salt, the fact that you have a lot of meat doesn't really mean very much.

So pretend you are in the old markets of Mali and trade away!

Towns begin to spring up in the Sahel.	People master making iron.	One million people live in the Sahel.	Kingdom of Ghana rises in Africa. Roman Empire falls.	Ghana is
2750 B.C.	500 B.C.	A.D.200	300-500	

HOW IT ALL BEGAN

The rise and fall of Ghana (300-1150)

Over 3,000 years ago three very important things happened in western Africa.

The first was learning how to raise important crops—yams along the coast, millet (a grain like wheat) in the savannah, and rice in wet areas.

The second was learning how to make iron—and then, iron weapons and tools. An iron spear is more dangerous than a wooden one. An iron tool is stronger so farmers can till more land and grow more crops.

The third was the growth of trade. Mali became a busy crossroad connecting Europe, Asia, and the rest of Africa.

This is a book about ancient Mali, but to understand how Mali grew strong, we must first learn a little about a land to the west.

Between the years 300 and 500, a kingdom called Wagadu grew strong. It became known as **Ghana** (GA-*nuh*), which means "warrior king."

The Soninke, the people of Ghana*, had lots of food and weapons to protect themselves. They were peace-loving and gentle. They had kings who were smart and brave. And the people of Ghana mined gold—lots of gold—so Ghana grew rich.

But a time came when long periods with no rain dried up two vital rivers. Food grew scarce, and the weakened country was attacked by invaders from the north. By the the year 1200, Ghana was a shadow of what it had once been, but to the east, a new empire was growing stronger every day. That country was Mali, which means "mighty hippo."

OLD SOLDIERS

The sculptures on these two pages are more than 700 years old! Warriors were some of the most important people around, and archers and horsemen the most powerful.

The griot tells us, "*Old kings die. New ones are born. And in the land of Mali, things were about to change.*"

* NOTE: *The modern country of Ghana lies 400 miles to the southeast of the ancient kingdom and was named to honor it. See page 45 for a map of the Ghana empire.*

Chapter Five

SUNDIATA

Son of the Buffalo and the Lion (1210–1260)

You now know a little about the ancient lands of Ghana and Mali, but you must also learn about one more event that happened far away in what is now Saudi Arabia.

In the year 610 a man named Muhammad had a powerful dream that led him to start a new religion called **Islam** (ISS-*lahm*). He dreamed of a world where rich and poor are equally loved by God. His teachings caught on quickly, and over time his followers traveled across Africa, bringing their new faith with them.

The Mande peoples, and other groups in Mali, had prayed to the great spirits of nature for thousands of years, but as word spread of a new faith, many became **Muslims**—people who follow Islam.

As more and more Arab traders came to West Africa, they brought their faith, laws, and ways of doing business with them. The religion of Islam was spreading, so it came to pass that a mansa of Mali decided to become a Muslim. Naturally many of his subjects decided that if their king was doing it, it had to be good.

But some people did not want to give up their old ways. Around 1230, a man named **Sumanguru** (*Soo-man-GOO-roo*) of the **Soso** peoples, decided that the time was right to take over the mansa's throne. Sumanguru was power-hungry. He wanted all the gold and salt. He made people pay high taxes. He had his enemies killed and forced their wives, mothers, and children to become his slaves. He was very cruel.

The Mande peoples needed someone bold to lead them. But who would it be?

The griot stands up and smiles, *"You have heard of George Washington. You have heard of King Arthur. The people of Mali needed someone brave to lead them to freedom. Now you are about to hear the wonderful tale of a real-life Lion King!"*

"You have heard of George Washington and the cherry tree—a tale that teaches us that honesty is very important. In Mali, children hear such legends about their great kingdom's beginning and learn lessons of bravery…and hope. Here is one version of that famous tale."

One morning two men came to the court of a powerful mansa. With them was a very ugly woman, a hunchback named **Sogolon** (SO-*guh-lawn*). The strangers told the mansa that he must marry this woman, for she had the spirit of a mighty buffalo—a powerful creature—within her. The mansa married her, and a year later they had a son whom they named **Sundiata** (S*un*-JAH-*tuh*), which means the "Lion Prince."

It is told that on the day of Sundiata's birth, a great storm swept across Mali. Bolts of lightning shot across the sky. The wind howled. "It is a sign," the griots said. The power of the buffalo and the power of the lion had joined together in this child. But there was a BIG problem.

The mansa already had a wife, **Sassouma** (*Su-SOO-muh*), and a son, **Dankaran Touman** (*Danka-ran • TOO-man*). The mansa's first wife hated Sogolon and the baby, and she began to plot against them. To add to the trouble, something wasn't quite right with Sogolon's little boy. As the years passed, he could not walk, he could not talk, and his head was way too big! Had Sassouma poisoned him? The mansa loved his son, but everyone made fun of a seven-year-old who could only crawl. The first wife was always laughing at little Sundiata, comparing him to her own beautiful, strong son.

When the mansa died suddenly, his first wife made Sogolon move. Even though the king had named Sundiata as his heir, Sassouma got the royal council to place *her* son, Dankaran Touman, on the throne. She sent Sundiata and his mother to live in a horrible little hut.

Do you remember Sumanguru? It was at this time that his army came into Mali and took control. Sassouma said she would be loyal to him, so he spared her and her son. And Sundiata surely was no threat! Sumanguru laughed and said the Mande people were weak, just like the crippled son of their old, dead king!

The Griot plays a beautiful melody on his kora, and his eyes sparkle, *"Something caught fire in Sundiata's spirit. Something strong filled his heart. Something amazing was about to happen!"*

One morning, Sundiata's mother sat crying. The evil queen had made fun of her boy once again! Sogolon grew so sad that she started hitting poor Sundiata, yelling at him to walk. Sundiata ordered his griot to go to the blacksmiths and bring back the strongest iron pole they had. It took six men to carry it. With every ounce of strength he had, Sundiata planted the heavy pole into the ground, gave a huge cry, and stood up. The thick iron pole bent like a bow with his effort!

A fat-trunked baobab tree

Then an even more amazing thing happened. Sundiata walked over to a **baobab** (BAY-*oh-bob*) tree and pulled that mighty tree right out of the ground! He carried the huge tree to his happy mother as a gift, for the tiny leaves were a much-prized spice. The young lion prince had roared!

Within the next few months Sundiata grew very strong. But Sassouma had other plans. She wanted Sundiata dead.

The griot's voice grows loud, "*First Sassouma sold Sundiata's dear griot to the wicked Sumanguru. Then the evil queen went to the Nine Great Witches of Mali and ordered them to kill the boy. But the witches found they had no power over a person with a pure and gentle heart. They tried to kill him, failed, and gave up.*"

Sundiata learned that Sumanguru believed that the spur of a rooster's foot would undo the magic that gave him power, so Sundiata had a special iron arrow made. He tipped it with a poison made from the blood of a white rooster stolen from Sumanguru's camp. Then he took a piece of the rooster's spur and attached it to the arrow.

At just the right moment Sundiata took careful aim and fired. His arrow struck Sumanguru in the shoulder. When Sumanguru saw the rooster spur, he screamed in horror and rode off into the hills. He was never seen or heard from again, and his armies, now with no leader, ran away.

Mali was saved, and Sundiata returned to the place of his birth to became his country's king. Good things were coming!

Chapter Six

THE BRIGHT COUNTRY

Niani: palace of gold

Imagine a place where most people live happily. No one goes without food, and people treat one another with kindness. It is safe to walk the streets at night. There is music in the air and storytellers to listen to. There are games to play and markets full of yummy food.

LET'S MAKE A DEAL

Modern-day buyers and sellers meet at Djenne's great Mosque (MOSK)— a place for Muslim prayer. The scene is little changed from 800 years ago, as people noisily haggle over prices.

This was the way it was in the land that Sundiata made strong. From his royal palace, **Niani** (Nee-AH-nee), Sundiata ruled with a golden heart. He was a wonderful mansa, and he was well-loved. He was kind, funny, and wise. Other kings came to him for advice. He treated poor people the same way he treated rich ones—with kindness and respect.

One legend says that Sundiata often wore the clothing of a simple hunter. He invited the sons and daughters of other mansas to come and live in his palace. He believed that it was good for his children and the children of other kings to grow up as friends. Friends never attack their friends, do they?

Under his rule Mali grew rich. Merchants and traders felt safe. There was peace in the land.

The griot plucks the strings of his instrument and sings a song that the children of Mali sang long ago,
> "He has come • And happiness has come.
> Sundiata is here • And happiness is here."

Sadly, around 1255, after many wonderful years as king, Sundiata died. The griots have many stories about how he passed away. Some say he drowned. Some say he was hit by a stray arrow at a festival. What would happen to the Bright Country?

Chapter Seven

THE GREAT KING

Mansa Musa and his gilded empire (1307–1337)

After Sundiata's death his son Mansa Wali took over. He was called the Red King because his skin was the color of copper. He ruled for fifteen years, and during his time Mali grew richer still. But the kings who followed in his footsteps were terrible. One even went mad and started shooting arrows at his loyal subjects.

The griot stares at the brilliant sky, and his eyes grow bright, "The Kingdom of Mali needed a strong leader. The grandson of Sundiata's half-brother was just the person for that job. His name was Mansa Musa and, oh my, he was an amazing man."

Mansa Musa became the greatest of all the kings of Mali. In other parts of the world they called him "The King of Africa," and he came to rule a vast empire—almost as large as all of Europe!

MUSA'S MAP

This portrait was part of a map drawn in Spain in 1375. Because a European drew it, he drew the wrong kind of crown. Mansa Musa always wore a gold skull cap or a turban of gold cloth.

Mansa Musa divided Mali into **provinces** (PRA-*vin-siz*), which are a lot like our states. Each had a governor. Each big city had a mayor. There were royal tax collectors at each marketplace and a huge army to keep the peace.

The whole of the Sahel—the great "shore" of the Sahara—was covered with trading routes. Long camel caravans brought news of the world and all sorts of wonderful products through the crossroads at Mali. There was very little crime, and everyone felt safe. There was so much gold that Mansa Musa, seated upon his golden throne and protected by a huge silk umbrella, could do almost anything he pleased.

Mali was growing bigger and stronger. Mansa Musa turned his sights on a new place—**Timbuktu** (TIM-*buck-too*). This city had first been settled around 1100 by a woman named Buktu, of the Amazigh people. While grazing her herds, she found an **oasis** (*oh*-A-*sis*) with cool, sweet water and lots of shade trees. She decided she liked it there. Soon her little camp became known as Buktu's Well. The word "tim" means "water well."

Timbuktu was near the Niger River at the place where the river turns north, bringing it closest to the Saharan trade-routes, so it soon became an important stopping spot for the caravans. Merchants began to build markets and homes. By the time Mansa Musa began to rule, Timbuktu had grown into an amazing city.

A caravan draws near to Timbuktu. This engraving was made in 1853, about 500 years after Mansa Musa's rule.

The griot crouches by the river's edge. "Now, Mansa Musa loved books and learning. While he was king, Timbuktu became known not only as a city of gold and salt, but as a city of books. Its university, Sankore, grew bigger. And some of the smartest, most talented people in the world came to teach and write and learn within its walls."

Timbuktu had become one of the richest cities on Earth. Soon there was a second university. There were over 170 other schools! The great library was filled with precious books from far away lands. Timbuktu was indeed the "Pearl of Africa."

TEATIME IN TIMBUKTU

There is a special way to drink tea in Mali. Why not try it? Pour some unsweetened tea into a cup. Add some mint. Take a sip of it. It tastes quite bitter. Now add a 1/2 teaspoon of quick-dissolving sugar. It is a little sweeter, right? Now add another 1/2 teaspoon of sugar. The tea tastes great!

Your first sip is a symbol of the bitterness of death. The second sip is a taste of the sweetness of life. The third sip is the delicious taste of love!

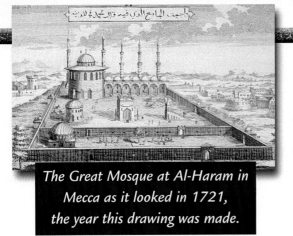

The Great Mosque at Al-Haram in Mecca as it looked in 1721, the year this drawing was made.

Mansa Musa was a very devout Muslim. One thing that every Muslim must do at least once in his or her lifetime is visit a city called **Mecca** (MEH-*ka*), where Muhammad, the man who founded Islam, had once lived.

Mecca is in Saudi Arabia—a trip of more than 3,000 miles from Mali—across many places with no roads. Can you imagine riding a camel from New York to Texas? In 1324, Mansa Musa set off on this very special trip, which is called a **hajj** (*hodge*).

A modern day visitor to the pyramids wears traditional style clothing to protect against the hot sun.

The griot laughs, "So, *off he went, taking 500 slaves with him! Each slave carried a six-pound staff of gold. Following behind the slaves were one hundred camels, each loaded down with 300 pounds of gold! A hundred more camels followed behind, piled high with food and clothing.*

Sixty thousand people followed Mansa Musa on his trip—a journey which took eight months."

One of the places Mansa Musa stopped was in Cairo, Egypt—the land of the great pyramids. He stayed for several months and spent money like mad. He gave gold to beggars in the streets. In fact, he gave away so much gold that its value dropped because there was simply too much of it floating around. When there is too much of anything, it is no longer very valuable. For ten years after his trip, gold was not worth very much at all in Egypt.

AND THEN THE KING SAID...

Much of what we know about Mali comes from the diaries of a famous Muslim explorer named Ibn Battutta (IB-in Bah-TOO-ta), who spent a month living in the court of Mansa Musa. He kept very detailed notes about what he saw, ate, and did.

33

MIGHTY MUD

You might think of mud as an odd thing with which to build. But mud can be really strong. Some buildings in Mali have been standing for more than 500 years although they must be repaired often. And in case you didn't know it, our own bricks are simply mud and sand baked in a special oven.

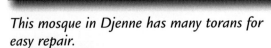

This mosque in Djenne has many torans for easy repair.

When Mansa Musa returned from his journey to Mecca, he began to build even more. The most beautiful structures he ordered built were great mosques or **masjids** (MAS-*jeedz*)—places for Muslim prayer. In America people live, work, and pray in homes of wood, brick, or stone. In Mali there were very few trees. There were very few rocks. But there was plenty of earth, so that's what people used to build their homes—wet earth and mud bricks mixed with ground-up rock, covered with clay.

For most of the year this works very well—that is, until the summer rainy season starts. Heavy rains can wash away a building just as waves can wash away the sandcastles you build at the shore. So architects set wooden beams into the mud to form ladders called **torans** (TOE-*ranz*) so that it was easy to repair the buildings when they started to wash away.

BUILD A CASTLE MALI-STYLE

You will need some very wet sand or mud, a few small plastic bowls and cups, and about twenty-four twigs or popsicle sticks. Study the pictures of the buildings in this book and try to build in that style.

Push the sticks gently through to make ladders. Do they make the building any stronger than one built without twigs or sticks?

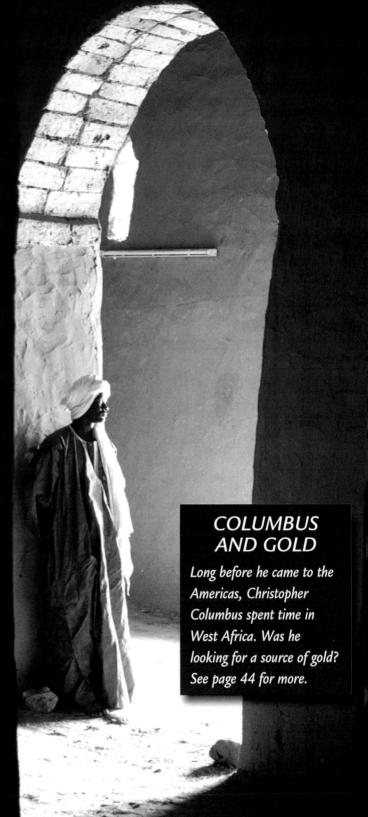

Thick walls keep the insides of Mali's great mosques cool.

COLUMBUS AND GOLD

Long before he came to the Americas, Christopher Columbus spent time in West Africa. Was he looking for a source of gold? See page 44 for more.

The griot's eyes grow sad. *"You now know, my children, that nothing lasts forever. In 1332 Mansa Musa passed on to the next world, and his son took his place on the throne. But his son did not have his father's wisdom or his father's good heart. It was the beginning of the end."*

Timbuktu was attacked again and again by the **Mossi** (MOH-*see*) people, who lived east along the Niger River. Mali was no longer a safe place, and the traders grew scared. Two princes who had come to live in Mansa Musa's palace left and went home to the city of Gao. They used their knowledge of Timbuktu to start a new kingdom that would soon conquer Mali.

Mali had no more strong leaders. People began to cheat and steal. Traders were afraid to come to the markets. By 1500, something else was happening.

As European sailors learned how to build strong boats that could cross the oceans, the old caravan routes slowly became useless. These sailors knew all about West Africa's gold, so they sailed down the coast of Africa and set off to find the gold fields by themselves. Mali no longer controlled the gold trade.

In time fewer caravans came to Mali. The land also grew drier as the climate changed. And Mali—once so very rich—grew smaller and less powerful.

The griot sighs, *"As one door closes, another opens. And as the foundations of ancient Mali began to crumble, a new empire was rising."*

Civil War begins in Mali.	Timbuktu is attacked by Berber warriors.	A weakened Mali is overtaken by Songhay.	Sunni Ali becomes king.
1359	1433	1450	1464

THE LAST KINGDOM

The Songhay Empire (1464–1591)

Just as Mali drew its strength from the Niger River, so too did the **Kingdom of Songhay** (SONG-*hi*) and its capital city, **Gao** (GOW). Gao lies about 260 miles east along the river from Timbuktu. But it had its own ways, beliefs, and kings.

Songhay's rulers had learned many lessons from the empire of Mali. Some had even spent their young years living as guests in the palaces of Malian kings. As Mali fell upon bad times, the kings of Songhay made sure their lands stayed safe for the caravans.

DESERT STORMS

The Tauregs, one of a group of people called Berbers, live in North Africa. They live much the same way as they did hundreds of years ago. Covering their faces protects them from blowing sand.

Sunni Ali captures and destroys Timbuktu.	Seven-year siege of the city of Djenne ends.	Sunni Ali dies. Columbus sets off to America.	First Africans are taken to America as slaves	Morocco overtakes Songhay.
1468	1466-1473	1492	1518	1591

In 1468 a Songhay king named **Sunni Ali** (SOO-*nee* AH-*lee*) captured and almost destroyed the city of Timbuktu. He then set off to take the city of Djenne. He surrounded the city and starved the people into surrender. After seven long years the king of Djenne gave up. The Songhay empire now ruled Mali's lands. The great empire of Mali was gone.

The Songhay kings would rule until about 1591, when Gao was overrun by invaders from Morocco— warriors with something new and terrible—guns. For the next 300 years each tried to capture and then sell their enemies to slave traders. Columbus' discovery of the Americas and Europe's mastery of the seas changed things, too.

By 1897 the French had taken control of all of what had been Mali, but by then there was a new enemy— the climate. Year after year it grew drier as less rain fell. Mali's days of glory had passed forever.

The griot rises to his feet. The sky has grown dark. *"You have heard stories of salt, sand, struggle…and of course, gold! You have learned of great kingdoms that are now memories. But Mali's might lives on in the stories of the griots. And they live on in the dreams of the great-great-great-great-great grandchildren of the strong people who built mighty cities on the "shore" of the desert."*

Chapter Nine

MALI TODAY

What lies ahead?

What is it like in Mali today? There are no more rich cities, but people still live rich lives, filled with wonderful traditions.

Bamako (BAH-*ma-ko*) is the modern-day capital of Mali. It is a poor city, but visitors say that the people are cheerful and kind—a tradition they carry with them from the days of Sundiata, the Lion King.

In 1897 France took control of Mali, and today, even though Mali won its independence in 1960, French is still the official language. But Mali is a bit like America in one very important way.

These Tuareg boys keep their faces covered. In their part of the world, it is considered rude for males to show mouths in public. Men wear veils, women do not.

A Fulani woman

A Dogon man with a ceremonial mask

A Bambara girl

In America people from different backgrounds live together—Latinos, Chinese, Italians, African Americans, Native Americans…and so many more. Mali is the same.

You can see some of the many faces of Mali here. The **Tuareg** (TWA-*reg*) boys on the left still lead camels across the desert. The **Dogon** (DOH-*gone*) people live in the hilly part of Mali and are known for their colorful religious ceremonies. The **Fulani** (Foo LA-*nee*) are fine herdsmen and farmers. The **Bamana** (BA-*muh-nuh*) are the biggest group. There are more than twelve major ethnic groups in Mali today!

The legend of Sundiata is still told with pride. The memory of those golden years still shines like a bright star in Mali's memory.

And what about the griots? Are they still important? Of course! They still strum the strings of their koras at weddings and celebrations. Some of the hottest pop music stars in Africa are griots! And why shouldn't they be? After all, what can be more important than learning about the past to help make a better future?

41

TIMELINE

1,000,000 B.C.E*–Early people develop in Africa. They have fire, simple tools, and the ability to speak.

60,000 B.C.E–People have already moved out of Africa to all parts of the world.

8000 B.C.E–The Niger River area is settled.

500 B.C.E–West Africans learn to make iron.

146 B.C.E–429 C.E–The empire of Rome extends into North Africa (the modern-day countries of Algeria, Morocco, Tunisia, and Libya).
Berbers, a small group from that area, start moving south across the Sahara.

200 C.E.– About one million people live in West Africa.

500–The Kingdom of Ghana grows rich from trade in gold and iron.

610–632–Muhammad creates the religion of Islam, which spreads after Arabs conquer North Africa and Spain.

700-1000–Ghana is the strongest nation in western Africa.
Europe is torn apart by long wars and disease.

About 1085–Ghana is invaded. Trade is almost completely stopped.

Followers of Muhammad spread news of Islam

*B.C.E. means Before the Common Era. The year 1 in our modern calender marks the Common Era. Dates are sometimes noted as B.C., for Before Christ and A.D. for Anno Domini, which is Latin for Year of our Lord, which mark the years since the birth of Jesus Christ. Since there are so many religions in the world, most historians use B.C.E. instead of B.C. and C.E. instead of A.D.

1150–The Soso attack Ghana.

1235–Sundiata defeats the Soso and builds a new kingdom in Mali.

About 1255–Sundiata dies. Mali is the center of the gold/salt trade.

1307–Mansa Musa takes the throne of Mali.

1324–Mansa Musa makes his trip to Mecca, stopping in Egypt.

1325–Mali captures the land of Gao.

1332–Mansa Musa dies.

1350–The Black Death sweeps across Europe, killing one-third of its people.

1433–Timbuktu is attacked by invaders from the North.

1450–Mali becomes a part of the Songhay Empire.
In Europe, a new period begins the Renaissance—a rebirth of the arts, sciences, and learning.

1464–Sunni Ali begins his rule over the Songhay Empire.

1492–Sunni Ali dies.
Columbus makes his voyage to America.

1591–After repeated attacks and civil war, the Songhay empire is attacked by Morocco. Slave traders bring ruin to the area.

1619–First Africans come to Virginia Colony as indentured servants.

Berber warriors

Events in
Europe

Events in
the Americas

43

THINGS TO THINK ABOUT

☞ **Some believe that the people of Mali had ocean-going boats and came to America long before Columbus.** A natural current runs through the Atlantic Ocean from the middle of Africa's west coast almost directly to the place where Columbus landed in 1492. Did Columbus learn about a route to the Americas from his years working in Africa as a trader?

☞ **Where is Niani?** Archeologists (ARK-*ee-ol-ah-jists*) are people who dig up old cities and historic places. They are still doing "digs" at Sundiata's palace which is in modern-day Guinea (see map).

☞ **What do Italy and Mali have in common?** Gold! Many tons (a ton is 2,000 pounds) of West African gold made its way to Italy during the **Renaissance** (REN-*a-sonce*)—a period of time known for great progress in art and science. Mali's gold was used in paintings, sculptures, money, and on churches.

☞ **Slavery has been a part of life for a very long time, and there were slaves all over the world in times past.** Skin color had nothing to do with slavery. It was only when the Atlantic slave trade began in the late 1500s that mostly black-skinned people were captured.

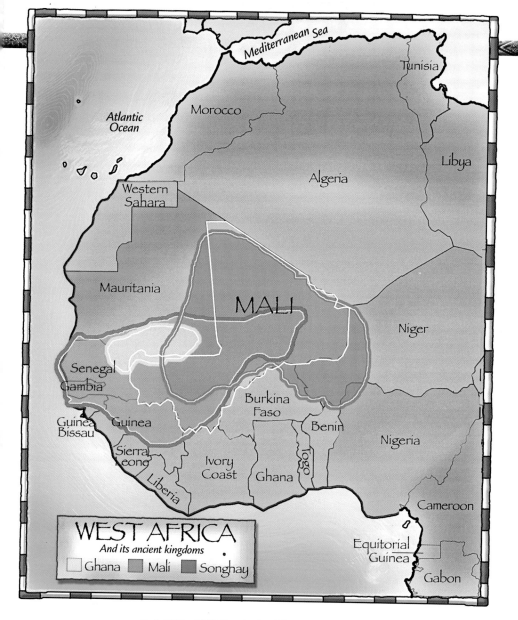

Map labels:

Mediterranean Sea

Tunisia

Morocco

Atlantic Ocean

Libya

Algeria

Western Sahara

Mauritania

MALI

Niger

Senegal

Gambia

Burkina Faso

Guinea Bissau

Guinea

Benin

Nigeria

Sierra Leone

Ivory Coast

Liberia

Ghana

Togo

Cameroon

Equitorial Guinea

Gabon

WEST AFRICA
And its ancient kingdoms

☐ Ghana   ▨ Mali   ▧ Songhay

WEST AFRICA'S ANCIENT KINGDOMS AND HOW THEY COMPARED

This map of modern-day West Africa shows the three great
empires and the lands they once controlled.

INDEX

REFERENCES
AND RESOURCES

BIBLIOGRAPHY

Clarke, Leon E. *Through African Eyes, Vol.1, The Past.* New York, NY: CITE Books. 1988. HS

Connah, Graham. *African Civilizations.* Cambridge University Press. 1987. ADULT

Mann, Kenny. *Ghana, Mali, Songhay: the Western Sudan* (African Kingdoms of the Past). Parsippany, NJ: Dillon Press. 1996. MS

"Mansa Musa King of Mali." *Footsteps African American History,* September/October 1999, Vol. 1, No. 4. MS

McKissack, Patricia and Fredrick: *The Royal Kingdoms of Ghana, Mali, and Songhay.* New York, NY: Henry Holt and Company. 1994 MS

Niane, D.T. *Sundiata. An Epic of Old Mali.* Essex, England: Longman African Writers. 1965. HS

Wisniewski, David. *Sundiata Lion King of Mali.* New York, NY: Clarion Books. 1999. ELEM

VIDEOS

Africa: The Story of a Continent. Written and presented by Basil Davidson: RM Arts. "Caravans of Gold" V2

ONLINE

www.vmfa.state.va.us/mali_geo_hist.html
Focuses on the art of Ancient Mali and includes a list of curriculum-related resources.

www.bu.edu/africa/outreach
Resources for K-12 teachers: lesson plans, teaching advice, video rentals, teaching kits and more.

www.nmafa.si.edu/educ/mali/index.htm
A good source with many related links from the Smithsonian Institute

A NOTE FROM THE AUTHOR

The fictional griot who serves as a narrator throughout this book speaks not only of Mali's Kings, but also touches on the history of the Kingdoms of Ghana and Songhay. A real griot in Mali would never speak of other kingdoms. Also, griots usually regale people in the marketplace or in a crowded courtyard. To create an air of mystery, I moved the setting to the shore of the River Niger and made the group smaller and more involving in the hopes that children will feel as if they are sitting at the feet of a master storyteller. I hope I have succeeded.

There are many different versions of the Sundiata legend. This book's retelling is based on the version by D.T. Niane called *Sundiata. An Epic of Old Mali.* In addition, it is very difficult to reconcile the geography of an ancient realm, whose borders existed in the days before maps were commonplace, with the modern-day nation of Mali. The ancient empire of Mali spread over several modern countries: Mali, Guinea, Senegal, Gambia, and Guinea-Bissau as well as Mauritania, Burkina Faso, and Cote d' Ivoire.

Front cover photo:
Typical Malian architecture—the world famous Mopti Mosque

Shown here: The Great Mosque at Djenne